My Home Country

COSTA RICA

IS MY HOME

For a free color catalog describing Gareth Stevens' list of high-quality books, call 1-800-341-3569 (USA) or 1-800-461-9120 (Canada).

For their help in the preparation of *My Home Country: Costa Rica*, the editors gratefully thank the Friends (Quaker) Peace Center in San José, Costa Rica; Professor Michael Fleet, Marquette University, Milwaukee; Professor Howard Handelman, University of Wisconsin-Milwaukee; and Professor Cecilia Rodriguez, University of Wisconsin-Waukesha.

Flag illustration on page 42, © Flag Research Center

Library of Congress Cataloging-in-Publication Data

Foran, Eileen.
        Costa Rica is my home / adapted from Ronnie Cummins' Children of the world--Costa Rica by Eileen
Foran ; photographs by Rose Welch.
            p.   cm. -- (My home country)
        Includes bibliographical references and index.
        Summary: A look at the life of an eleven-year-old girl and her family on their farm in Costa Rica. Includes a section
with information on Costa Rica.
        ISBN 0-8368-0847-9
        1. Costa Rica--Social life and customs--Juvenile literature. [1. Family life--Costa Rica. 2. Costa Rica. 3. Farm life--
Costa Rica.] I. Welch, Rose, ill. II. Cummins, Ronnie. Costa Rica. III. Title. IV. Series.
F1543.8.F67   1992
972.8605--dc20   92-17727

Edited, designed, and produced by

Gareth Stevens Publishing
1555 North RiverCenter Drive, Suite 201
Milwaukee, Wisconsin   53212, USA

Series editor: Beth Karpfinger
Research editor: Kathleen Weisfeld Barrilleaux
Cover design: Kristi Ludwig
Layout: Kate Kriege
Map design: Sheri Gibbs

Printed in the United States of America

1 2 3 4 5 6 7 8 9 96 95 94 93 92

My Home Country

COSTA RICA
IS MY HOME

Adapted from Ronnie Cummins'
Children of the World: Costa Rica

by Eileen Foran
Photographs by Rose Welch

Gareth Stevens Publishing
MILWAUKEE

Eleven-year-old Cristiana lives in a mountain village, where she works on her family's small dairy farm and in their modest restaurant. She attends Escuela Lourdes, an elementary school near her home. Cristiana enjoys riding her horse along the Sacramento mountain trails.

To enhance this book's value in libraries and classrooms, clear and simple reference sections include up-to-date information about Costa Rica's history, land and climate, people and language, education, and religion. *Costa Rica Is My Home* also features a large and colorful map, bibliography, glossary, simple index, research topics, and activity projects designed especially for young readers.

The living conditions and experiences of children in Costa Rica vary according to economic, environmental, and ethnic circumstances. The reference sections help bring to life for young readers the diversity and richness of the culture and heritage of Costa Rica. Of particular interest are discussions of Costa Rica's unusually stable government and its commitment to peace among its Central American neighbors.

My Home Country includes the following titles:

Canada	*Nicaragua*
Costa Rica	*Peru*
Cuba	*Poland*
El Salvador	*South Africa*
Guatemala	*Vietnam*
Ireland	*Zambia*

CONTENTS

LIVING IN COSTA RICA:
Cristiana, Life on a Farm

Eleven-year-old Evelyn Cristiana Gonzáles-Hidalgo lives on a farm in Sacramento, Costa Rica. Cristiana lives with her parents, Obdulio and Ana Beliza, her brother, Uriel, and her sister, Olga Patricia. Cristiana likes living in the small village. Everybody knows each other, and many people are related. Cristiana's uncles, aunts, and grandparents all live nearby.

Cristiana, her parents, and brother, Uriel. Olga, Cristiana's older sister, is away at school. ▸

The family never tires of the view from their Sacramento home.

Obdulio is a carpenter for a hotel near Sacramento.

Cristiana's Home and Family Farm

Cristiana lives on a small dairy farm that has cows, chickens, turkeys, geese, and horses. In the back of the house, there is a fruit and vegetable garden. Attached to the house is a restaurant, where the family cooks homemade meals. Cristiana's father is a carpenter. He built their five-room house with the help of relatives and friends.

Ana Beliza manages the family restaurant.

Uriel works on the farm.

Cristiana helps where she can.

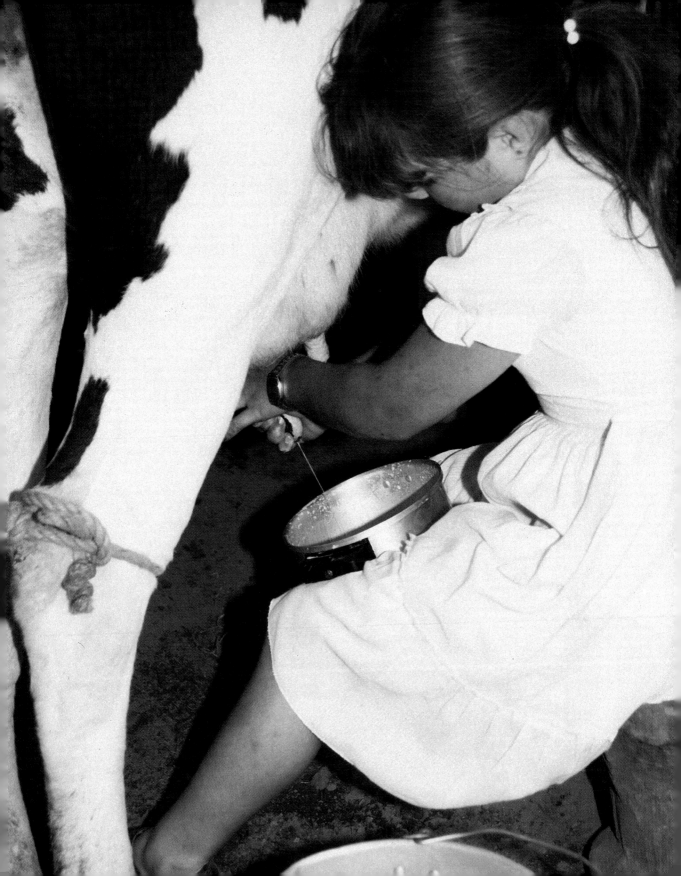

A Typical Morning for Cristiana

Cristiana wakes up when it's still dark outside. She gets dressed, then brings in the cows from the pasture. She feeds, washes, and milks each cow by hand.

Cristiana learned to milk the cows when she was just seven years old. Now she can milk a cow as well as most adults.

◄ **It takes strong hands to milk the cows.**

**Left: Cristiana takes fresh milk back to the house, where breakfast is waiting.
Below: Cows graze in the pasture all day long.**

13

**Cristiana's waiting breakfast.
Below: Selecting firewood . . .**

By 6:30, Cristiana eats breakfast. She usually has rice, black beans, fried *plátanos* (bananas), and a cup of *café con leche* (coffee with milk). A hot breakfast tastes good after working in the chilly morning air.

School starts at 11:00 a.m., so Cristiana has time for other chores. First, she splits firewood. Sometimes, Uriel and Cristiana have a contest to see who can split the most wood. Cristiana likes this game, and often wins!

. . . and splitting it. ▶

After splitting wood, Cristiana feeds the chickens, turkeys, and geese, and then her puppy, Caballito. The name *Caballito* is Spanish for "little horse." When Cristiana finishes her chores, it's 9:00 a.m., and time to get ready for school.

Cristiana likes feeding the turkeys, geese, and chickens.

Cristiana puts on her school uniform — a blue skirt and a white blouse. Cristiana doesn't mind wearing a uniform to school — she is used to it! Most Costa Rican schoolgirls wear a similar uniform.

Cristiana feeds Caballito.

Cristiana shines her shoes.

Having her hair brushed relaxes Cristiana!

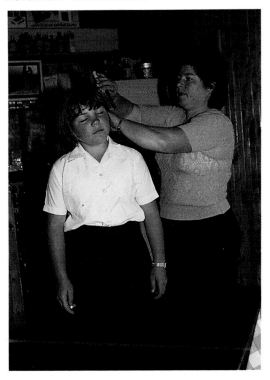

Cristiana's Elementary School

Escuela Lourdes is just a short walk from Cristiana's house. The two-room schoolhouse has only 30 students and one teacher. Cristiana goes to school nine months a year and has vacation in November and December. Cristiana's fourth- and fifth-grade class has three boys and eight girls, including her friend, Liliana. Together, they study subjects like math, science, history, reading, writing, geography, and art.

◀ **Cristiana takes the shortcut to school.**
Below: Cristiana and her classmates pose with Don Melvin Chavéz, their teacher.

Cristiana's teacher is *Don* Melvin Chavéz. (In Spanish, the use of *Don* or *Doña* before a first name is a sign of respect.) Don Melvin has planned a trip to a nearby rain forest. He tells the students how important it is for Costa Rica to protect its rain forests. The rain forest fascinates Cristiana, so she looks forward to the class trip.

Cristiana and Olga talk about the fun things they do at school.

**Above: Cristiana displays her textbooks and notebooks.
Right: Cristiana's classmates find the areas where rain forests grow.**

Don Melvin talks about Costa Rica's vanishing rain forests.

At recess, Cristiana's classmates like to play *policía y ladrónes* (cops and robbers). Before classes start again, the children eat a quick snack. Usually, they have a fresh fruit drink and a corn tortilla.

Left and below: The trees and bushes around the school make good hiding places.

Above: Cristiana and Liliana wash up after recess.
Below: A midday snack.

Unlike many other countries in Latin America, Costa Rica uses a lot of its money on education and very little on weapons or defense. When Cristiana reads about wars in the world, she is proud that her country abolished its army in 1948.

Below: The students wait in line to wash their dishes.

A Farm Visit

Cristiana often visits her grand-parents' farm. Her great-grandmother planted a flower garden there years ago. Cristiana likes gathering flowers to take to her mother.

Cristiana and her grand-mother enjoy being together.

Cristiana cuts flowers to decorate the restaurant.

On weekends, Cristiana and her grandparents milk 20 cows by hand. On weekdays, Cristiana's father and her Uncle Martin help. They use milking machines to keep the milk fresh and clean.

Below: Uncle Martin strains milk through a cheesecloth.

25

Cristiana and Pajarito go to meet the milkman.

Cristiana and the family horse, Pajarito, deliver the milk to the milkman. Pajarito carries the milk in metal jugs on his back. Cristiana helps the milkman put the milk on his truck.

The milkman gives Cristiana empty milk containers in exchange for the full ones.

A plate of pastries.

Uncle Martin joins Cristiana
for something to eat.

Cristiana's grandmother has made bread,
fresh cheese, and pastries just in time for a
break. Cristiana eats quickly, then turns on
the radio. Her favorite songs are in English
and are recorded in the United States.

Cristiana listens to some of her favorite songs.

A sign for La Campesina.

Ana Beliza prepares dinner for hungry travelers.

La Campesina

Obdulio built the family restaurant. *La Campesina*, Spanish for "the country woman," is popular with both local people and tourists. Dishes include soups, shish kebabs, *flan de coco* (coconut custard), and fresh sour cream and tortillas.

The whole family works together to run the restaurant and the farm. Cristiana often helps her mother in the kitchen and has learned many cooking skills.

During the week, the restaurant is not very busy. But on weekends, people crowd the restaurant.

Above: The restaurant menu hangs where everyone can see it.

Right: Cristiana keeps the dining area clean.

Many people passing through Sacramento are on their way to Braulio Carrillo National Park, which is just 2.5 miles (4 km) away from the Gonzáles farm. Cristiana thinks many people come to their restaurant for the beautiful view of Costa Rica's central valley. At night, thousands of lights twinkle in San José below.

Below: The colorful lights of San José flood the valley.

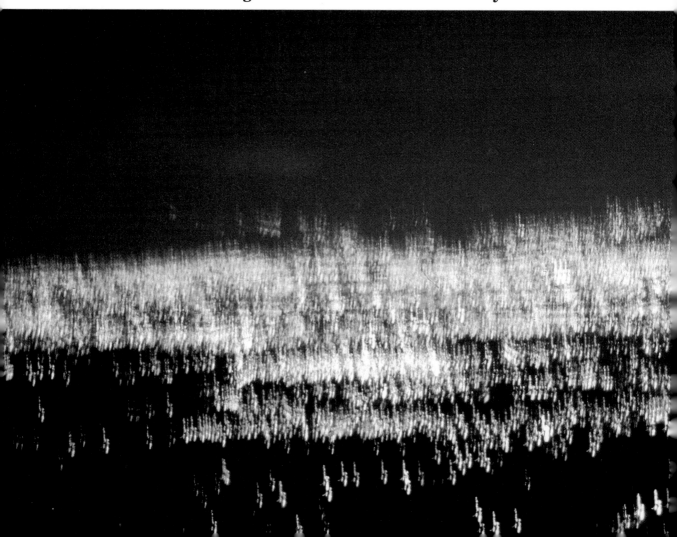

Cristiana's father is building an outdoor patio so the customers can enjoy the magnificent view. Cristiana and Uriel help their father.

Right: Obdulio works on the patio.

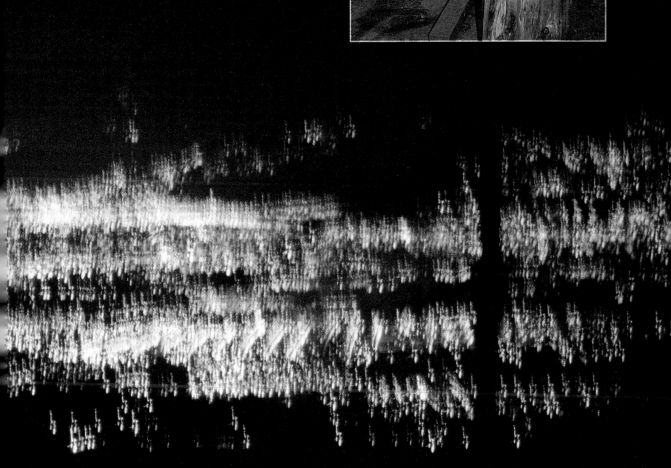

Today, without being asked, Cristiana cleans her room.
◀ **Cristiana loves to ride Pajarito.**

Cristiana's sister Olga goes to school in
Heredia, which has a population of 30,000.
Cristiana likes to go to the shops, movie
theaters, and the swimming pool in Heredia.
In three years, Cristiana will go to junior
high school there. She can hardly wait!

Corn tortillas, fresh sour cream, and café con leche.

Shish kebabs.

La Campesina is known for its mouth-watering desserts.

Heredia's tropical fruit stands attract many buyers.

Typical Foods of Costa Rica

Sacramento markets can't carry every kind of food, so Cristiana's family goes to Heredia for tropical fruits, such as bananas and pineapples. Traditional Costa Rican foods include tortillas, rice, beans, potatoes, eggs, and fruit. These foods are used for breakfast and lunch. Dinner foods include a meat or cheese dish and a fresh salad. Tonight's dessert is flan de coco.

Sunday in Sacramento

Sundays are quiet in Sacramento. Like many Costa Ricans, Cristiana's family belongs to the Roman Catholic church. Sacramento's small Catholic church is on the mountainside, not far from home.

Cristiana arranges flowers around the church altar.

Everybody listens as the village priest begins the Mass.

Everyone is eager to get to the national park.

A Trip to the Park

Cristiana and her friends hike along a forest trail.

At Braulio Carrillo National Park, Cristiana explores the rain forest. She knows that many animals and birds live in the forest. Her father has taught her to identify many of them.

37

After eating lunch on top of the Barva Volcano, the children play hide-and-seek and hike along a forest trail, where they see many kinds of plant life. They make sure not to wander too far into the thick forest. No one wants to get lost in such a dark, strange place!

By the time they get to the truck, everyone is tired. No one notices the bumpy ride back to school.

Above: Don Melvin explains how to use a compass.
Left: Cristiana and a friend feel the leaves of a huge fern growing along the trail.

Above: Everyone eats lunch.
Left: Tortillas filled with sausage, egg, and cheese.

Right: Cristiana is "it."
Below: Melon is for dessert.

Above: Cristiana's tree.
Below: Small sticks protect
the trees from animals.

Planting Trees

After visiting the National Park, Cristiana's class decides to plant trees in the schoolyard. Each student is responsible for one tree.

Cristiana imagines what her tree will look like when it is grown. She hopes that by the time she is an adult, all people will value Earth as much as she values her little tree.

Cristiana and a friend water the trees. ▶

MORE FACTS ABOUT: Costa Rica

Official Name: Republica de Costa Rica
(ray-POOH-blee-kah day
KOHS-tah REE-kah)
Republic of
Costa Rica

Capital: San José (SAHN hoe-SAY)

History

In 1502, Christopher Columbus came to Costa Rica. Sixty years later, the Spanish arrived and enslaved the native Indians, who soon fled or were killed by disease, hunger, and warfare. But in the 1600s, the Spanish lost interest in the area.

By 1838, Costa Rica was free of Spanish rule, and Braulio Carrillo Colina became president and dictator. Under Colina, the economy and population grew. But rebels, unhappy with the dictatorship, forced Colina from power. After many years and revolts, Costa Rica made a new constitution and declared itself a republic. In 1855, William Walker, a U.S. citizen, invaded Costa Rica. In 1856, in the Battle of Rivas, Walker's army was defeated and Costa Rica became independent. Today, Costa Rica is one of the most peaceful and prosperous nations in the world. The government provides health care, social security, and public education for all.

In 1987, Costa Rica's then president, Oscar Arias Sánchez, won the Nobel Peace Prize for promoting peace in Central America. Costa Rica, a country with no army, is considered a model of democracy.

Land and Climate

Costa Rica, which is northeast of Panama and south of Nicaragua, has coastlines on the Carribean Sea and the Pacific Ocean. It is the second smallest of the Central American countries. Costa Rica is a fertile land with a warm, mild climate. In the highlands, the average temperature is 72°F (22°C). On the coasts and lowlands, the average temperature is 81°F (27°C).

People and Language

People of European (mostly Spanish) descent make up about 87% of Costa Rica's population. Spanish is Costa Rica's main language. English is also taught as a second language. The Indian languages have almost disappeared.

Education

Costa Ricans are among the best educated people in Latin America. Children 7 to 14 must go to school. Over 90% of the people go to high school. The University of Costa Rica is the largest institution of higher learning in the country.

Religion

Almost 90% of Costa Ricans are Roman Catholics. The remaining 10% of Costa Ricans are mostly Protestants and Jews.

Sports and Recreation

The most popular sport in Costa Rica is soccer, but baseball, basketball, tennis, and track and field are also popular.

Costa Ricans in North America

Thousands of Costa Ricans visit the United States and Canada each year. But few move there. They like living in their own small, friendly, and prosperous country.

Costa Rican coins and paper money.

Glossary of Useful Costa Rican (Spanish) Terms

café con leche (kah-FAY KON LAY-chay): coffee with milk.

Don (dohn): title used as a sign of respect for a man. *Doña (DOHN-yah)* is used for a woman.

flan de coco (FLAHN DAY COH-coh): coconut custard.

More Books About Costa Rica

Costa Rica. Carpenter (Childrens Press)
Fodor's Central America. (McKay)

Things To Do

1. Find out more about Costa Rica's rain forests. What is being done to save them?

2. If you would like to have a pen pal from another country, write to: Worldwide Pen Friends, P.O. Box 39097, Downey, CA 90241.

Be sure to tell them what country you want your pen pal to be from. Also include your full name, age, and address.

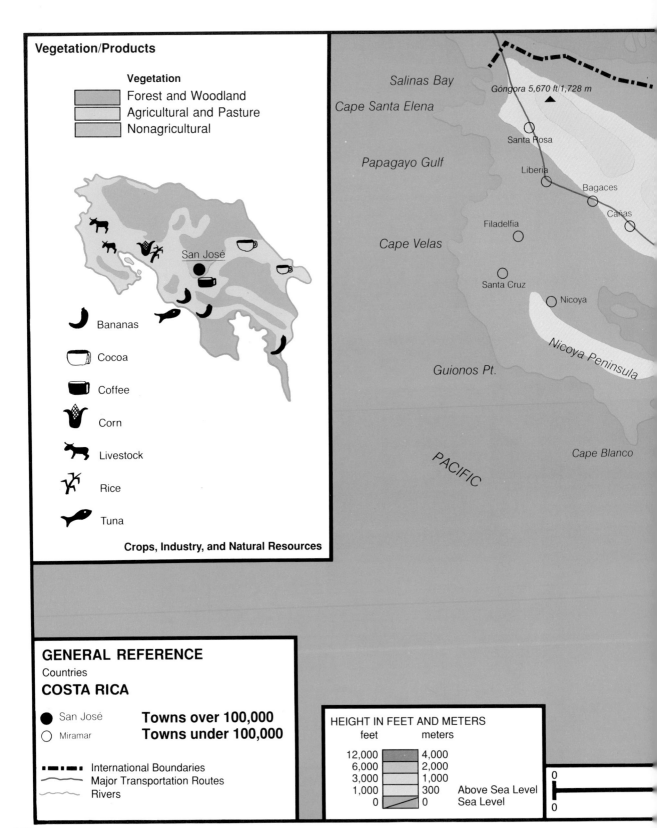

Vegetation/Products

Vegetation
- Forest and Woodland
- Agricultural and Pasture
- Nonagricultural

San José

- Bananas
- Cocoa
- Coffee
- Corn
- Livestock
- Rice
- Tuna

Crops, Industry, and Natural Resources

Salinas Bay

Cape Santa Elena

Góngora 5,670 ft/1,728 m

Santa Rosa

Papagayo Gulf

Liberia

Bagaces

Cañas

Filadelfia

Cape Velas

Santa Cruz

Nicoya

Nicoya Peninsula

Guionos Pt.

PACIFIC

Cape Blanco

GENERAL REFERENCE
Countries
COSTA RICA

- ● San José
- ○ Miramar

Towns over 100,000
Towns under 100,000

- ▬▪▬▪▬ International Boundaries
- Major Transportation Routes
- Rivers

HEIGHT IN FEET AND METERS

feet	meters
12,000	4,000
6,000	2,000
3,000	1,000
1,000	300
0	0

Above Sea Level
Sea Level

0

0

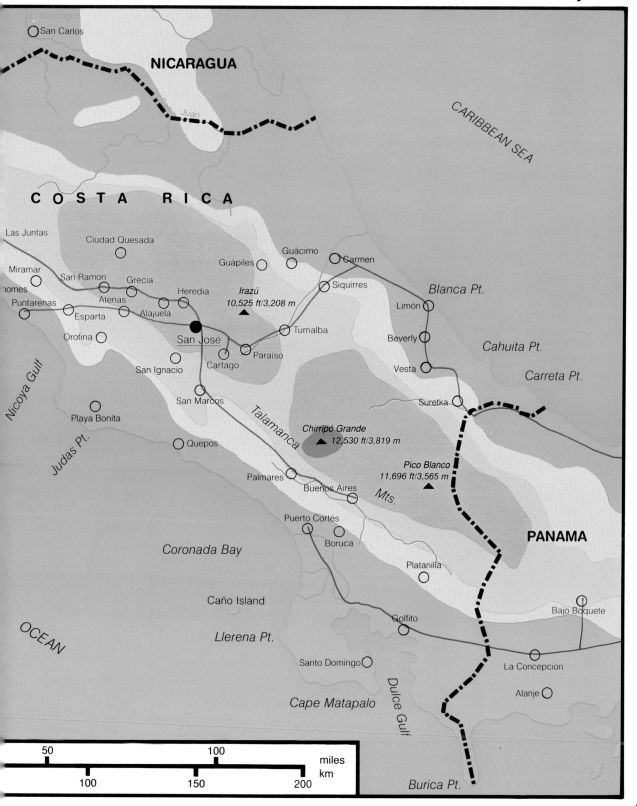

San Carlos

NICARAGUA

S. Juan

I. Nicaragua

CARIBBEAN SEA

C O S T A   R I C A

Las Juntas

Ciudad Quesada

Guácimo

Guápiles

Carmen

Miramar

San Ramón

Grecia

Siquirres

Blanca Pt.

nomes

Atenas

Heredia

Irazú
10,525 ft/3,208 m

Limón

Puntarenas

Esparta

Alajuela

Turrialba

Beverly

Cahuita Pt.

Orotina

San José

Paraíso

Vesta

Carreta Pt.

San Ignacio

Cartago

Suretka

San Marcos

Talamanca

Chirripó Grande
▲ *12,530 ft/3,819 m*

Playa Bonita

Pico Blanco
11,696 ft/3,565 m
▲

Nicoya Gulf

Quepos

Palmares

Mts.

PANAMA

Judas Pt.

Buenos Aires

Puerto Cortés

Coronada Bay

Boruca

Platanilla

Bajo Boquete

Caño Island

Llerena Pt.

Golfito

OCEAN

Santo Domingo

La Concepcion

Cape Matapalo

Dulce Gulf

Alanje

50	100

miles

100	150	200

km

Burica Pt.

47

Index